Bullies:

Monologues

on

Bullying

for

Teens and Adults

by

Jim Chevallier

Second Edition

Copyright © 2011, 2014 by Jim Chevallier
published by **Chez Jim**

These monologues are works of fiction. Names, characters, places, and incidents are products of the author's imagination or are used fictitiously. Any resemblance to actual events or locales or persons, living or dead, is entirely coincidental.

PERMISSIONS, ROYALTIES AND MODIFICATIONS

These monologues may be used for workshop, audition, and classwork purposes without royalty consideration. Individual monologues may also be performed royalty-free in presentations where the majority of the work is by other authors. However, if more than ten monologues by Jim Chevallier are performed before an audience where admission is charged, or if the performance is primarily promoted as being from this collection or by this author, royalty payment is required. Prior permission is required for any form of recording or broadcast, including but not limited to radio, television, video, motion picture and Internet.

Contact the publisher for applicable rates and permissions. E-mail (**jimchev@chezjim.com**) is the best way to do this. You may also visit **www.chezjim.com** for the most current contact information.

Performers are welcome to make minor changes in gender, context, length, etc.

NOTE TO THE SECOND EDITION

This edition includes a number of additional monologues for teens written since the first edition.

Table of Contents

Introduction

"I've tried being other people and being me suits me best."
Chris Colfer (*Glee*)

In the mid-Nineties, a group of bullies at an English girls' school put feces in a thirteen-year-old's bed. That was only one of the things they did to her before she changed schools. Why? Apparently because she was too tall and had eczema.

A few years later, in New York, others took a young woman they'd been tormenting and threw her in a trash can.

In 2011, the first victim, Kate Middleton, married Prince William and became the Duchess of Cambridge. The second, Lady Gaga, already at the height of her success, put out an anthem - "Born This Way" - for all who are different. Yet in a documentary she is seen, tired and discouraged, wondering if she will always be the girl who got thrown in a trash can.

The duchess and the "lady" are only two of the many people who have succeeded brilliantly in life after surviving bullying in high school. Often, as with Middleton's height, people are bullied for one of the very things that makes them stand out later. So many people discover that, like the ugly duckling in the folk tale, they never fit in with the ducks because... they were a swan.

But to do that, you have to survive.

2011 was also the year that two fourteen-year-olds hung themselves because they could no longer stand being bullied. Tragically, they are only two in a long list of teens who could not look beyond the pain of a brief period in their lives to see how much larger, how much better, Life could be.

Yet every adult who has experienced bullying themselves yearns to tell thousands of tormented teens who cannot imagine anything beyond the taunts, the blows, the rumors inflicted on them by their peers this one thing: **it gets better.**

And it does.

But you have to survive. More than that, you have to keep alive inside you the very thing that so many bullies try to destroy, the very specific, individual thing that makes you... different. Perhaps someday, if you are true to it, different like Lady Gaga and the Duchess of Cambridge. But one way or the other, specifically and uniquely yourself.

It would be nice to say that there are no bullies in college or in the adult world. But of course there are. All through Life you will meet people who are strong in one way – physically, intellectually, financially – but feel terrifyingly weak in another, and so use whatever strength they have to make others feel smaller, to reassure themselves that they are not as weak and afraid as they feel inside. This may be a boss who berates his subordinates; it may be a colleague who undermines others; it may be (increasingly) some anonymous person on the Internet. No one can tell you honestly that bullying ends with Senior Prom.

Still, most of us find it easier later in Life to deal with such people; to stand up to them, or change jobs, or simply ignore them. When you are younger, when you have not yet seen enough of Life to know how large it is, how much more there is to it; when you feel vulnerable and alone, it is different; it is often overwhelming. Most adults know that; many remember it.

The present collection explores this all-too-common experience from the point of view of the bullied, the bullies, the people who do or don't help, the people who are marked by the experience, the people who triumph, the people who don't. Some of these are clear-cut, classic cases of bullying: people being beaten up or mocked, having things stolen. Others are cases where people may say something that belittles or humiliates someone else, or does them professional harm, without any obvious ill will. Yet the other person may never forget the effect of their words.

Like any collection of monologues, this one seeks to give voice to all those involved, to offer actors an opportunity to embody them, but also to, if not educate, at least inspire those who read them to consider the many sides of this question: what people suffer and what people survive, what prompts people to torment others and what people do or don't realize about their own actions; what all this costs in the short or long term.

Many voices speak here, about many different experiences. But to the degree that this book has any one message, it is that our individuality, our uniqueness, is never a liability, no matter how hard it can sometimes be to remember that, and that the more we keep it in view, the more we honor it, the more likely we are, not only to survive, but to triumph.

"Your heart's pounding, you sweat, and you feel like you're going to vomit...I just laid it down. I don't like bullies."
Tom Cruise

"If people can look at me and see that I was one of those bullies that always made fun of gay people, and I had this huge secret, so there's always a bigger story than what you see."
Lance Bass

"I'd eat my lunch in the nurses' office so I didn't have to sit with the other girls. Apart from my being mixed race, my parents didn't have money so I never had the cute clothes or the cool back pack."
Jessica Alba

"I was bullied and it's hard, you feel like high school's never going to be over."
Megan Fox

"They would also write things on the sidewalk in permanent marker. They really hated me."
Jessica Simpson

"When I would ask them why..., they would just say, 'Well, you're fat."
Demi Lovato

"I got beat up just about every day."
Chris Rock

Are YOU being bullied?

Are you a teen who is being ***bullied?***

These are only some of the sites which offer help:

- Stop Bullying - www.stopbullying.gov

- Bullies: What is Bullying? - pbskids.org/itsmylife/friends/bullies

- Dealing With Bullying - kidshealth.org/teen/your_mind/problems/bullies.html

GLBT teens in particular should visit the It Gets Better Project at www.itgetsbetter.org

High School (Teens)

Long Way Home

If I take the long way home, they won't see me. But I have to be quiet. If they spot me, they'll come after me. Then I'll have to run. Which makes them laugh. They like that, that I'm scared. The more scared, the better. It's like a game: the more scared I am, the more points they get.

Fun. All kinds of fun.

It's probably my fault. I must have done something. To make them think I was fair game. Some creature made to be chased; a creature whose natural state is scared.

I know it's something about me. Something wrong. Maybe I could change it if I tried. If I could only figure out what it was.

It's not like I don't have time to think. I've got lots of time when I'm taking the long way home. Hugging the wall. Keeping my head down.

Trying not to be scared. Trying so hard not to be scared....

Refinements

I could hurt him. I could hurt him bad. But I don't.

In fact, I hardly hit him at all. Little taps; a thump on the back. A hard thump, so he can feel it. But not so's it'll hurt him. Nah.

Enough so's he's scared, is all. Just at the sight of me, way up the hall. Hoping I won't come towards him. Hoping I won't get close. And if I do get close, right up on top of him, so's he has to look up at me – even when he's trying hard to pretend I'm not there, even then I can see him. Like a cat with its ears drawn back, hair standing up. Hoping for one thing; his heart beating with one hope.

That I won't hurt him.

And mostly I don't. Sometimes I just stand there for a long time, then enjoy his relief as I walk away.

See what I'm sayin'? It's an art. It's got techniques, refinements. You have to perfect your style.

'Cause don't get the wrong idea, it's not like I'm some kind of crude bully. I'm an expert. Expert at what I do.

Examples

Here's what I've figured out: everyone's got a weak spot, something they hope that no one will notice. Me, I notice. But I don't always talk about it. Sometimes just enough to let them know I could talk about it. But that's for the dangerous ones, the ones who could hurt me.

Some, I'm not afraid of. Them, I'll talk about.

They're my examples.

Here's a for instance. Buster, who everyone's afraid of? He sees a doctor. A special kind of doctor. Do I know what kind? No. I just know his office is by the cupcake shop, the pricey one downtown. One day my mother went there and left me in the car. Who do I see but Buster, being dropped off at the building next door. It's only doctors. I checked. Mind doctors, mostly.

So a few weeks later, out of the blue, he starts in on me. "What's your problem?" I say. "Those cupcakes got you wired?" He stops cold. "Cupcakes? What the – ?" "You know, like they sell at that place downtown." You should have seen his face. Dead white.

That's all I said. But he knew. He knew I could say more. Because of what happened to Martin.

Martin's smart. But book smart; not smart like me.

He was trying to be my friend. So I let him. Long enough to learn stuff – like about his mom. His mom brings guys home while his dad's at work.

I waited until he really, really trusted me, until he really thought I was his friend. Then I told Hilary. Nobody likes Hilary. She's always talking about other people. But when you want people to know a thing, you tell Hilary.

Soon it was all over school. Texts, graffiti. And the Web page. There's always a Web page. This one showed Martin's mom. Some one stuck her face on a naked body, then added a bunch of guys all around her.

Martin doesn't talk to me now. Or anyone else. That's rough. I feel bad about that. I do. But you know what I feel great about? Buster knew how this got out – you can bet I made sure of that – and now he's scared of me. Plenty scared.

So I've got no worries when it comes to Buster. But does that mean I'm done? Done making examples? Not by a long shot.

You never know who else might come along.

Ugly

My dad says I'm beautiful. He says that all the time. But he's lying. I know he is. Because he's my dad.

I'm ugly. I know I'm ugly because the kids at school say I am. Even the guys. The same guys who take me places no one can see. Sometimes when we're there, they even make me feel beautiful; that's why I go. But after, when we're in front of people, when it's just kids joking around, they say it too. How ugly I am. And I believe it. Because everybody says it.

Why would they say it if it wasn't true?

My dad says they're jealous, that the girls only say it because they don't want people to notice how pretty I am, and that then the guys just go along. "But that doesn't stop them, does it?" he says.

"They still want to be with you when no one else is around. Don't you see? Don't you see they know you're pretty?" No, I don't see. They want to go with me just to have fun, and I let them have fun, because that's the only reason they'd be there. There where I get to feel beautiful. But after, when it's not just us anymore, they tell me the truth. That I'm ugly.

They wouldn't just say that, would they? Right in front of everyone?

Why would they say it if it wasn't true? Why would they say it just to be mean?

Mindy's

I didn't know he was Mindy's. I was new here. And he never told me. He always acted like it was just me and him. Like we were together. But not in front of other people. He said it was better not to cause talk, that he was private about these things. So how was I to know? To know that he was Mindy's. And that everybody knew that. Everybody but me.

But of course she found out and then someone told me she was angry and when I asked why, they said, "Like, duh-uh. He's Mindy's. Everybody knows that." And all of a sudden all her friends, which is like all the kids that matter, they all hated me too. Now even kids who don't know me, who've hardly ever seen me, even, they call me names. No one wants to eat with me or sit next to me. Someone even put tampons in my locker. Used tampons.

So I don't want to go to school. Not anymore. My mother says, "Oh honey, you just got there. You have to give the place a chance." But she doesn't understand. And I can't tell her. I can't tell her how bad it is. She'd just get upset and make things worse.

She thinks I'm just starting out, that it's just me being in a new school. "You've got your whole life ahead of you," she says. But she doesn't understand. She doesn't understand that my life is already over. I just got here and already my life is done.

Manners

My mother says manners are really important And one thing she always says is, "Don't be contrary. People like it better when you agree. See what everybody else thinks and try to stick with that. That's just good manners, to try to get along."

That's why people like me. I go along. And my friends. People like my friends too. Not that we're a clique or anything. People just like us, that's all.

Some people liked Audra, too, when she first came to school. But one of our friends didn't and so that was that; none of us did.

But the guys did. Brandon especially. And everybody likes Brandon. He's a big deal. Only he had had a few dates with my friend Kandi. So when he started dating Audra, we all got mad.

Then someone said we should get her back. For stealing Brandon. Maybe do something to scare her away. So of course I went along. Just like my mother taught me.

Kandi said she wanted to talk to her, out behind the school. Right by the woods. Then when Audra came to meet her, she said, "Let's go in the woods. It's more private." And when they did, we were all there waiting. We were just going to shove her around a little, maybe give her a few slaps. Only, there were a lot of us and things got out of hand. Because no one wanted to say, "Stop, that's enough." Because no one wanted to be contrary. But we never meant to hurt her. Not that bad.

When I see her in her wheelchair now, sure I feel bad. Maybe I should have said something; maybe I should have spoken up.

But you've got to understand: that's not how I was raised.

Collateral Damage

It's not like we beat her up or anything. We put up a Web site. With some jokes. That's all they were: jokes.

We never thought people would believe that stuff. Or start spreading it around. Or spray paint her car.

We didn't do that. Don't blame us.

I don't even know how it started, to tell you the truth. It's just like, I don't know, someone got annoyed at her and someone else made a few jokes and then someone, maybe me, I'm not saying it wasn't, I just don't remember, said it would be funny to put the jokes up on-line, only we needed to come up with some more, and when we did they kept getting meaner, we were just seeing how far we could take it, then by the time we put up the page, they were bad, they were, I can see that now, but at the time we were proud of ourselves, proud of how funny we were, and we couldn't wait to get this stuff up.

It's like it wasn't even about her anymore, it was about us, us showing how smart we were, and then, us being a group, too, a team, that felt really good, being part of something, like we were this special elite crew, this hit squad, and we felt powerful, we felt really strong, especially when the other kids began to pick up on it, then it was like, "Wow! We made our mark, we scored!"

So it wasn't about her, you see? It was about doing something, something people would notice.

When you come down to it, she didn't matter. She didn't matter to us at all.

Flowers

Don't think you could have helped. You couldn't have. And it's too late now. Or it will be by the time you read this. There's only one thing left you can do for me. This is how I want my funeral:

For the music, check my phone. I left a playlist on it. It's marked "Send-off". Some of it's sad, like you'd expect, sad and soft. But a lot of it is loud. Because it's what I'd use to drown out those words, the words I heard people whisper, the words I read on-line. The words that kept shoving at me, telling me to go. Telling me no one wanted me around.

The words that put me here.

And I want flowers. White flowers. Lots and lots of white flowers. White, for purity. Because no matter what they said, no matter what pictures they posted, I was always pure. Pure inside. So show them, show them how I was inside. Show them with mountains of flowers, white flowers; show them what they destroyed.

You'll want to talk about me. Of course you will. What a good daughter I was. How much you loved me, how special I was. How much you'll miss me. Forever. You'll miss me forever. Do that. Say all that. Let everyone who loved me stand up and say that, say it so they'll hear.

But then it will be their turn. Melanie, Samantha, Sarah. Their turn to speak. I want them to get up, one after the other, and say they're sorry. Sorry for what they posted. Sorry for what they whispered. Sorry for what they made me into. What they made me in people's eyes.

And after they've said that, standing up there surrounded by all those white flowers, by the purity they stained and crushed and destroyed, I want them to say they're ashamed. Ashamed they made me do this. I want them to say that in front of everybody, so everybody will know exactly who they are. Exactly what they are. Because they'll have said it, said it in their own words. The same words they used to taunt and torment me, to hound me into a corner. A corner with no hope or light.

A corner which left me only one way out.

Fans

I'm on TV. I get fan mail. You might say I'm famous. At least for my age.

But it's not like I talk about that. I try to be normal, like any other high school kid. I try to be nice to people. And not just the popular ones. Everyone. I treat everyone the same.

So why do people hate me? Kids, I mean. The kids at school. Why do they think I'm stuck up, that I think I'm better than them? I know they think that. I know because I hear it in the hallway; I read it on-line.

Even when I smile at people and try to be friendly, I read later on what a phony I am, how nobody's fooled. That I'm just doing it for my image. But I'm not. I want to make friends.

I don't want to be lonely, every single day at school.

Today this reporter came and she set up in a classroom with her crew so they could do an interview. You know, "the star at her high school, just plain folks". The kids were all excited, trying to get a look at her. Because she's pretty well-known. I'd forgotten to bring a magazine, one with my picture on it, so before I went to make-up, I went to get it from my car.

Only when I got to the parking lot, I smelled something, something bad. Then I saw it was on my car: dog... poop, all over the windshield. And on the handles, and the wheels. With a big note stuck to it: "Because you think you're such hot...."

I went back inside and right to the make-up lady and didn't say a word. I just wanted to forget it. To keep my head in the game.

Only once I sat down and the lights were on me and that reporter was sitting across from me with a big smile, aiming her microphone right at me, the first thing she said was, "So, here we are in your high school, where, a year ago, you were just one more student. They must be really proud of you, no? You must be really popular." And all of sudden I broke down, just lost it completely. And then I ran off. Because I couldn't say, "No. No, the fact is they hate me here. Hate me for doing well. And it's great to be on the cover of a magazine. And it's great to be on TV. But I'm still just a kid, you know? And I just want what every other kid wants: to be liked, to have friends."

"What does the rest of it matter if you can't have that?"

The List

Sometimes I sit and list all the ways I don't belong. The clothes I can't afford, the car I don't drive, the bands I've never heard of. And so on.

Because the list goes on for pages. I keep thinking I'm done and then someone will walk by talking to someone else about something I know nothing about, some new hang-out, some new video on-line, and I'll think, "Oh yeah, that. I should write that down too." Or I'll see a kid with a new phone, one I didn't even know was out, and wonder how their parents can keep buying them the latest one when my parents had to wait forever to get me one nobody's ever heard of.

And so I write all that down too, about the phone, but also about our parents, and how mine aren't like other peoples', and about money, too, which kids always say doesn't matter, but of course it does, the things you get with it, they matter, especially to kids, and I write down all the things and all the thoughts and all the ways I'm not like anyone around me, and, yes, sometimes it gets to be a very long list, but the best thing is I know I'll have lots of time to write it, because nobody, absolutely nobody, is going to come up and interrupt me, it's a safe bet no one will be saying "Hi".

The Ant's Answer

I had this dream once where I was invisible and I tripped. Right there in the hallway, with everybody hurrying by. And they kept stepping on me. I'd cry out but no one could even hear me. They'd just keep hurrying, hurrying on. Stepping all over me.

That's what school's been like for me. If anyone noticed me at all, it was to give me a hard time. Like he used to. But even then I didn't matter. He and his friends would have their fun and then... be on their way. Once they were done, they'd forget all about me.

It's like when I was little and I'd tear ants into pieces just to see if the pieces could walk. Once I was done, I really didn't care where the pieces went. That's how people were with me. They'd tear me up, just for fun, and then move on.

Only, I couldn't move on. I was stuck with me. And no one to rip apart. Not with my hands anyway. Not even with my words.

How do you use words when no one hears you?

So I used what I had. On him and his friends. And now everybody's saying what a nice guy he was. And his friends. Great kids.

Me? Most people wonder who the hell I am and where I came from. That and what's the matter with me, I guess.

But there's one thing they don't do. Not now.

They don't ignore me.

Clicking

The party sounded like so much fun. Tyler played with his band. I like Tyler, but he doesn't know that; I doubt he even knows I exist. The party was in a big house. A big house with a pool. And all the food was gluten free; that's the big thing now. Everybody's eating gluten free. Even me. Not that anyone cares what I eat.

Just like no one invites me to parties.

I only heard about this one because Caitlin, who sits next to me, was whispering to Melanie, who sits on the other side of me and then Jenny, who's in the next row down, joined in. I think they forgot I was even there.

At least at first. Then Jenny glanced at me – I think she thought I wouldn't see – and pointed to her phone and everybody stopped talking. Out loud at least. Instead, they all started texting. All I heard then was the clicking and sometimes the giggles when someone wrote something funny.

I sat between the three of them as they texted each other about the party and laughed and sometimes looked up at each other to smile, smile about something they could all see on their screens.

They weren't ignoring me, exactly, it's more like they were in a world where I didn't exist and in their world they were remembering the party, remembering it all together, while in mine I was just listening to the clicking, the clicking and the laughter, and wishing I had something, anything at all, to remember.

Different

I wish I could be like everyone else. But I'm not.

So what do I do about it? Keep my head down? Hope they don't notice me?

'Cause they will, you know. They'll notice you when you're different. It's like there's a scent. Something in the air. The moment you come in you can see their nostrils widen, you can see their lips curl. They'd hurt you if they could. If they thought they'd get away with it.

Mostly they avoid you. Shrink away. Or make jokes. Ugly jokes.

Because they're afraid.

Isn't that it? As scared as I am of them, aren't they scared of me? Because I'm different. They don't know how to deal with that. They don't.

Sometimes I entertain them. Act silly, put on a little show. Sometimes it works, too. Everybody laughs. Even me.

Anyone who saw us would think we were having a good time. A great time.

They'd never guess I'm scared of them. Or even less that, deep down, they're scared of me.

Because I'm not like them. They don't know how exactly. Maybe in fact they're scared that I'm not that different. That beneath the surface they're just like me.

I understand that. I understand why they would be scared. Because I'm like me. I just am. And I don't want to be. I wish with all my heart I wasn't.

But I am. And the one thing I know for sure is, that's not going to change.

Somebody

Did you see how he dressed? How he acted? All the time. In front of everyone. Like, he wasn't even ashamed. Like he thought we should all accept him. Accept him like he was.

Come on. You know what my dad would do if I ever acted half as weird as that kid?

He'd let me have it, that's what he'd do. He'd let me have it good.

Because that's what you do when people don't act like they're supposed to. You let them know it. And how.

I tried too, tried getting in his face. And you know who got in trouble? Me. That's right, me.

Come on. Is that right? Because I was trying to talk to him? Trying to warn him?

It's not like anyone else would. They all acted like he was funny. Free entertainment. Some of the girls even liked him. The same girls who wouldn't give me the time of day.

But then I'm low-class, right? Me and my dad, we barely get by. I couldn't afford the stuff that kid wore. Not that I'd be caught dead in it.

But still. I'm normal. I'm regular. Why would anyone like him more than me?

Whatever. No one else saw the problem. Nobody else was taking action. So he thought he was fine. Fine just like he was.

And that was wrong. Just plain wrong. Somebody had to do something.

So, somebody did. Me.

Toadmouth

Why don't kids like me? Everybody likes you, right? And you're funny-looking.

Well you are. That's just the truth. Come on, no one's ever told you that?

But nobody calls you "Toadmouth". Or hacks your web page to show you with toads and snakes coming out of your mouth.

What's that about, anyway?

You get invited to parties. Think how that makes me feel – they'll even invite you, but not me.

Do you know how wrong that is?

I think it's because I'm smarter. I can't help that. Or that some of the other kids are so stupid. Hell, even when I try to help them out. They'll say something ignorant and right off I'll let them know. That what they said was dumb. You'd think they'd be grateful. Grateful that I'm teaching them something.

But the next thing you know, there they go again, saying exactly what I told them not to. Like they never even heard me. One kid, he even stopped saying 'hi'. Just took to walking right by me.

Can you believe that?

See? People don't like it when you're smarter. Except you. You don't mind, right? You still talk to me.

But then you get along with everyone, don't you? And you know why? 'Cause you're not threatening. No one takes you seriously. You just go along with whatever.

You're kind of lame that way.

Maybe it's because you lost your mom? Maybe that's it.

'Cause you know, losing your mom? That's big. That could really hurt your nerve.

I'll bet no one else has ever said that, right? See, because they wouldn't make the connection. Most kids here just aren't that smart.

Not even as smart as you. And you're not that smart.

But everybody likes you. And nobody likes me.

I don't get it. I don't get it at all.

Liked

It's not that I don't like you. Don't get me wrong. But the other kids don't – the kids who count. The kids I want to like me.

You can understand that, right? Wanting to be liked? Everybody does, right? Only, I don't know what it is, a lot of kids don't like you.

Don't ask me why. Seriously, I like you fine.

Don't ever say I said that. Because as far as they're concerned, I don't. I don't even talk to you. Nope, you're outside, in the cold. And I'm inside, where it's warm. One of them.

I like that, being warm. And safe. No one looking at me funny, no one making jokes about me they know I can hear. No one walking too close behind me in the hall. No one giving me the eye just to make me nervous.

No one treating me like you.

I'll bet you don't like it either. I'll bet you wish you could be one of us. Even me. And I'm right at the edge. I'm hanging by a thread. It would take a nudge, a flick to put me out where you are.

That's gotta be awful. I don't know how you stand it. And I wish I could help, I really do. But I can't. 'Cause I want people to like me.

You get that, don't you? You, of all people?

Mystery

There's things I just don't get.

I'm a weirdo. I know that. If I didn't before, I would by now, the way people treat me around here. It's like I smell bad. They can't get away from me fast enough. Like I've got some kind of disease. Even the kids who hassle me, they do their thing and then they're gone. Like they're afraid they'll catch it. Catch what I've got.

I get that. I do. Message received, loud and clear. I try to stay out of people's way, not sit too close to anyone at lunch. They want to act like I'm not there, I'll oblige. I'll do my best to be invisible.

'Cause you can get hurt. You can get hurt if people see you and wish they hadn't.

So, OK, that's me, nobody's friend; the outcast, the leper. That's the way it is. I'm not about to fight it. I learned long ago to face facts.

Only, you, you act like I'm normal. Like I'm like everybody else. You know you'll get grief for it, right? You know you'll hear words. Or worse. Much worse. But you still keep coming over to talk to me, like it was the most normal thing in the world.

Talking to the kid no one wants anything to do with.

So here's what I don't get, here's where I'm confused. Do you have some kind of blind spot? Do you just not care if you get cut out, if you end up on the outside – like me? Do you get some kind of thrill out of all this, out of going against the grain?

What I'm asking is, why aren't you like other people? Why can't you see what they do?

What I really want to know is: what's the matter with you?

Tough

"You're tough, right?" That's what Chelsea says. "Like a guy, almost." OK, maybe I am, in some ways. Like a guy. "You box, for godssake. How many girls box?" Which is right. I do. Put me in the ring and I can take a punch. That kind of pain I can handle. "It's so cool," she says. "It's like I can say just about anything, and it won't hurt your feelings." But the whole time I'm thinking, "Please. Please don't. Please don't feel like you can say just anything. Not to me." Still, Chelsea, well you know, she just goes on. "It's like you don't care that you're not pretty, or that some of the kids aren't comfortable having you around, you just let that stuff wash off." And I want to tell her to stop, to not remind me how I look or what people think of me, because I know all that; I've got eyes, I've got ears. And you know what? I've even got a heart. Which she could see if she was thinking. But she doesn't think, not much, not Chelsea, just keeps on talking, keeps on saying, "Because you're tough, you know, you can take it. You just don't care." And I want to tell her, "But I do, I do care. I care with all my heart and soul." But I don't.

I don't because I'm, you know, tough.

Big Help

You don't have to be so fat, you know. You could lose weight if you wanted.

I'm sorry if that sounds mean. But it's true. You're gross. I don't know why you bother to wear such nice clothes. It just draws attention. If I were as big as you, I'd hide it. I'd wear stuff that was baggy and dark, so that nobody would notice me. Aren't you embarrassed? Aren't you thinking to yourself, "I'm sorry, I'm sorry it's so disgusting to look at me"?

I'll bet you are. You act all smiley and confident, like you think you're fine like you are, that you look just like anyone else. But you don't, you know, not anyone human, anyway. Maybe an elephant or a rhino, dress a few of those up and bring them to school and then, oh yeah, you'd look right at home, you'd fit right in, no problem. Seriously why do you bother to eat lunch, you could skip a week of meals and still be good to go. But it's like you don't even try, it's like you think you're good just as you are, well, I'm telling you, you're not good, not good at all, and I'm sorry, I'm sorry if you don't want to hear that, but, come on, I'm just trying to help.

Stupid

Because she was stupid. That's why. That was the only reason.

Her mother's stupid too. How'd she fall for Sonny's trick? He made his voice go deeper, but you could tell. You could tell he was just a teen, not the assistant principal like he said.

"We need you to come in tomorrow, first thing in the morning. To talk about Colleen. Oh, and please don't bring your daughter." And she did it, that moron. She drove off, right after breakfast, and left Colleen in the house.

Alone. Just like we wanted.

She even left the door unlocked. Colleen was in her room, browsing the Web. She didn't even hear us. Not until I said, "What'cha doin'?" Just as sweet as I could be. Man, I'll never forget the look on her face, seeing me standing in the door.

And when she asked, "What are you doing here?" and I said, right back, "We're gonna kill you, bitch!", man, you should have seen her then. Oh, she was scared. Plenty scared. But she still must have thought we were joking.

Why wouldn't she? We'd pushed her around at school. Plenty. But never enough to leave any marks. She didn't even fight back; she never did. That's what made us mad.

That's what made us want to hurt her even more.

So, yeah, she was plenty scared. But still, I don't think she believed it at first. Not until Sonny started kicking her.

That part was fun, the kicking. I wanted to do it all like that, to finish her that way. But Sonny said, "We have to get out of here before her mom gets back." So he held her down and let me kick her in the face a few more times, but then, yeah, he made me choke her.

Made me do it quicker. I mean. It's not like he had to force me.

She still couldn't believe it. Even then. It wasn't like she'd done anything, the stupid bitch. It's like I said: she was just stupid.

I let her believe it too. A few times I stopped, just so she could think she had a chance. That I was just playing. But finally Sonny lost it. "Will you stop horsing around, Samantha?" And so I did it. I squeezed, squeezed hard, and kept squeezing until she believed it, really believed it. And then she went limp.

God, that felt good.

I never had any power. Not ever. Not even over my own dog. Mutt never listens to me. But I had power then. Oh yeah. I was on top of the world.

Anyway, I didn't think we'd get caught. Not so fast. You must think I'm pretty stupid too, huh? For dropping my ID?

Yeah, that was dumb. I guess I am pretty stupid.

Not stupid enough to be dead, though.

Best Friend

I'm her best friend, so I see it all. I was there after the crash when she lost her leg. I was there at her brother's funeral. It doesn't matter that he was driving; she still misses him everyday.

And I'm there now. After she gets the texts, I'm always there. The ones that make her cry. Or just scared. 'Cause some of them say: 'You're the one who should have died. And you will. Because I'm going to kill you." But it's the ones about sex that upset her most. "How's it feel doing it with only one leg, you whore?" That's what a lot of them say: "Whore, slut, tramp."

"I'm still a virgin," she said, just yesterday. And she fell into my arms, weeping her heart out. I tried to comfort her, stroking her hair, "I know, Honey" I said, "I'm your best friend. Don't you think I know that?"

The worst thing is, she can't imagine who could hate her so. She's tried guessing, telling me all the people she might have made mad. But she just can't think who would want to hurt her this much. She flinches when a text comes in, because she never knows if it might be another one. Another mean one. But it never is, not when I'm there. Still she gets so upset, trying to figure out who it might be. And the whole time I'm right there. I see it all, her terror and her tears, and she never dreams, never for a moment suspects, that the person sending the texts is me.

Crooked

You don't understand. I had to scare them, I had to make them think I was dangerous, that's why I bought it, so they'd know not to mess with me, so they'd take one look and go, "Oh no. That guy's trouble. We better keep away."

It wasn't so I could hurt anyone. I didn't mean for that, I didn't mean for that to happen at all.

Least of all, a teacher. Who expected a teacher to get involved? That was wrong, that wasn't in the plan. Only, don't you see, I was already scared, I was already on the lookout and so, when he came up to me, when he tried to take it away, well I just reacted, that's all, it's not like I even thought about it, it's just I was ready, ready for trouble like I always am, like I've been all year, ready for one of those kids to come up to me, and then whatever, because you never know whatever, you never know whatever happens next, which way to look, what to protect yourself from, and so, yeah, I brought it, and that teacher saw it, and he tried to take it away and I reacted, that's all, I reacted like I'd been ready to, every minute of every day, only it wasn't one of those kids, it was him, and I'm sorry, I'm sorry my fear got crooked, and the wrong person got hurt.

Not Even Me

I don't have to hurt, you know. I don't have to be scared.

I know a guy who'll get me beer and there's places I can go, like down the alley near our house or in the bushes by the highway, and I can drink and I can think about being someplace else, someplace where no one wants to hit me, no one wants to make fun of me, no one even knows I'm there. That's the best, the best of all, when nobody sees you, when you're invisible, because they can't hurt you if they can't see you and one day, maybe one day soon, I'll be invisible for real, I'll be gone entirely. Just let them try and get me then, let them try and wait for me or touch me or catch me, they won't have a chance then, because I'll be gone. But for now I can pretend, I can erase that person, that me that hurts, that person who can be hit. I can drink like some kid in a fairy tale, drinking a magic potion to become invisible, and then I won't be there, I'll be gone, I'll be lost where no one can find me.

No one. Not even me.

Revelation

You won't believe what just happened!

Robert – this is no surprise, right? – Robert started in on Brian. You know he was gonna, sooner or later. Poor Brian. He's a sweet guy, but he keeps trying to keep his head down, hoping no one will notice him. That's raw meat to a guy like Robert. I think he was letting him simmer, just letting him hope he wouldn't be on him the way he's on so many other kids. He's not that big, Robert, if you look at him, but there's something mean about him. There just is. Maybe just the fact that he likes being mean, that he really enjoys it. Like you never know what he might do.

So whenever he gets going on some kid, everybody else is so happy it's not them, they just stand away. They don't interfere. Then when he does get to them, when he's twisting their ear or backing them against a wall, maybe just really, really getting in their face, it's like they feel they deserved it, that they had it coming.

Who knows? Maybe I was one of them. I've certainly seen him do it enough. And not said a word. But he's never started in on me. Can't say why. Maybe it was just a matter of time.

So today, it was Brian's turn. Only, come on. Brian's a sweetheart. He wouldn't hurt a fly. So I lost it. I just did. "Leave him alone! What the hell's the matter with you?" I said. "Do you think this crap is funny?"

And Robert stopped. Stopped cold. Stopped and looked at me. Hard.

OK, I'll admit. I got a little scared. I was waiting for him to take a swing at me. Which, let's face it, would have been game over. Lights out.

Because no way am I a fighter.

Only, he didn't. He stood up straight and he looked at me and then around at everybody else. Like he couldn't believe it. He couldn't believe someone had called him out.

And then? He walked away. Just headed down the hall and out of sight.

Would you believe? That's all it took. Just one person, one person calling him on it and telling him he was wrong.

How come it took so long for me to figure that out?

High School (Adults)

The Closed Door

She goes into her room, closes the door and sits at her computer and you have no idea what she's looking at. Whom she's meeting.

Or thinks she's meeting.

She said she'd met a boy. On-line. It seemed harmless. Good, even. For two weeks, she was so happy. She'd come out humming and smiling. We both felt great, seeing her like that: light, for once, and carefree. Because she'd been so moody, we'd been worried. We even sent her to see someone.

But all at once she was over that. After she'd met this boy. That is, thought she had. Because they were always talking on-line, but never in person. Never face to face.

We didn't find out the truth until after. That he didn't even exist. "He" wasn't a he. He wasn't even her age.

This was an adult: one of her schoolmate's mothers. Can you believe that? Playing with her. Getting her back for something she thought my daughter'd said to hers.

And after she'd reeled her in, after she'd made her believe she'd found someone special, she brought the knife down. All at once, the "boy" turned mean. He told her she was trash, that everyone hated her.

I saw her come out in tears. But what did I know? It's the Internet. Half of what's on there is make believe. told her to forget it. I told her it was silly.

I told her she'd get over it.

Those were my last words. The last words I said to her, before she went back in her room and closed the door.

Lords of the Jungle

Look. Kids get bullied. That's part of high school. What are you gonna do? You can't be everywhere. They have to learn to fend for themselves.

Now granted these kids did go a bit far. Teasing's one thing, but when it gets physical, let me tell you, that's where I draw the line. You never know how that might end. Though it's not like they hurt him badly. No worse than what happens on the football field.

Why one of the same kids who roughed him up was in the hospital last year. With a concussion. You think he complained? Hell no. Never said a word. A week later he was right back in the scrimmage.

Because these are good kids. Fighters. Sure, they got a little rough. But young guys are rough, you know? It's that warrior gene. The testosterone. They want to feel their oats. Test their limits.

That's not all bad, either. I went to school with one of those kids' fathers. And let me tell you, he was just the same. Oh yeah, a real handful. But look at him now: raking it in. Because he's got that aggression. That drive.

Some of our kids are lions, is what it is. Lords of the jungle. Top predators on the food chain. And you can't expect a lion not to use his claws. That's just how it is.

Your son's... more like a herbivore. Not cut out for the competition. Oh I'm sure he'll find his niche, somewhere far from the fray. Someplace nice and safe. But let's face it, it's a rough world out there.

Sometimes people just get hurt.

Lovely Girl

You must understand, We all love Penelope: the other students, the staff. Everyone. She is the most delightful girl. Are you sure your daughter's not exaggerating? Oh, I know, girls can be thoughtless sometimes, hurtful, even. But to spread the kind of vile lies you're talking about, that's not like our Penny at all. And you know your own daughter, well, Winifer is a sweet girl, of course. But she is a little shy, you know, she doesn't mingle very well. I myself, I tried to talk to her, to draw her out, and, well, she's very guarded isn't she? Very watchful. Frankly, not to put too fine a point on it, she was very near to being rude.

That's not going to serve her well, you know, later in Life. It won't help her get on. Not at all. I don't want to be critical, you understand, but social skills are important and, well, to be honest, she doesn't have them. She doesn't... how can I put this?... She doesn't read other people very well. Isn't it possible, just possible, that she misunderstood what Penelope was saying, that she thought she meant more by it than she did? And that perhaps, it's possible you know, the other girls came up with the rest of it on their own?

Not that I'm doubting what you're telling me. And yes, of course, there are those texts. But it's just so surprising because I can't tell you enough, I simply can't say it too many times, how very much we all love Penelope. Simply adore her.

Parenting Skills

Wait a minute, you! Don't walk away from me!

Did you tell the principal my kid's a bully? Was that you? That he's been pushing your poor little darling around? Huh?

Where do you come off? What's the matter with you? Do you get off on causing trouble?

Don't you think you should think about that? Huh? Don't you think you should really, really think about that?

Look. They're kids. They do things. That's the way kids are. But they can handle it. They can work it out. If they've got any backbone, that is. If they don't expect Mommy and Daddy to come running every time they get a boo-boo.

What kind of kid are you raising anyway? What kind of parent are you? Aren't you ashamed? Raising a kid who can't stand up for himself? Raising a kid who's afraid of a fight?

Look, you want to bring up a wimpy little kid who can't even handle his own business, who can't give it as well as he can take it, who just bends over and takes it until he can run home crying, well, that's your business. That's just fine with me.

I'm not going to tell you how to raise your kid. But get this straight: nobody, not you or anyone else, nobody's going to tell me how to raise mine.

Lesson

Are you sure, Mr. Marshak? Are you sure you want to answer the question? I don't want you to embarrass yourself. It's admirable that you keep trying, but let's face it, you're not the sharpest knife in the drawer. I understand you might get flustered by people looking at you but it's not your awkward appearance you should be ashamed of, I'm not the kind of teacher to embarrass a boy about his weight, it's that you're always so eager to speak up and the truth is, I'm afraid, you'd really do better to listen and learn from your classmates, it's not your fault they're quicker than you and after all half the time when you do speak up, you make a complete fool of yourself, you do realize that, don't you? You simply wave your ignorance like a flag. So I'm giving you a chance is all, Mr. Marshak, do you really absolutely insist on answering the question or would you rather do yourself a favor and move to the back and keep quiet and hope nobody notices you?

It's your call, Mr. Marshak. It is absolutely your own call.

Torch

The last time someone snuck backstage? I let Security do the talking. There's some crazy fans out there. But I'm listening to you and it's not about talking to a star, is it? You want something else.

You want advice. You want to know how to get through it; how to survive high school when you're different...

Which, and never forget this, just means you're being yourself. People who do that, who stick to that, will always be different. Oh sure, some of us, we're different in a way that comes with a label, a label that's stamped crisp and clear in other people's minds. And that makes it harder. Because people have their ideas about that label. They won't see you as yourself: they'll see you as one of "them" – whatever "them" they have in mind.

But that's where it is, that "them" – in their mind. Always remember that. You're being you. Not anyone's label. Not anyone's idea of what that label means.

Not even your own.

Which is one reason it's so tough. Even with all that other crap. The things people do to you: the things people say. Even without that, just carving out that one little shape that's all your own, that doesn't fit any mold: that will never be easy.

But you know what? It's all you've got. In high school or after. It's the thing that will make you strongest, even if sometimes you wish with all your heart you could be like everyone else.

I did. No lie. There were days, I prayed to be "normal", to just be like everyone else. But look at me. Look at where I am now.

Because I cupped my hand around that flame, around that tiny flickering light, no matter how hard things got, and I carried it into the world and now it's a torch I hold up high. Crowds come to see my light shine.

And OK, I've got the money and my name in the papers and all those fans. But you know what makes me a success? The fact that I kept that flame alive, that I let it lead me even when I had to struggle to see it. I never let anyone else's hate define me or turn me down another road.

That's my success, right there. Take away the rest of it, I've got that. And you've got it too, tiny and fragile as it may feel now. Stay true to it, keep it alive, and one day you may find: you've got a torch to show the world.

Heart to Heart

That boy is scared, Matthew. To you and your friends, it's just a game. But your game makes him afraid to leave his house. His mother called me at work. She told me he hates school; that he's starting to fall behind in class.

Do you have any idea what that can mean for his future?

Do you enjoy this, seeing him trying to avoid you, trying to find a spot where you can't sit behind him and tug his hair? Or cut it. Didn't one of your friends do that? Cut off a bit of his hair?

I hope it was one of your friends. I hope it wasn't you.

You need to know this, son: when I was your age, I wasn't like you. I didn't have a whole group of friends. We didn't have much money, so I always wore old clothes. The kids at school, the kids whose parents did have money, just like I do now, after all these years, they judged me for that. And they didn't like me. They cut me out. And worse.

Much worse.

You get it? You see? That kid you're playing with, that kid you're pushing around, that could have been me.

And he might turn out OK; I did. I learned to fight back. I found my own friends. I figured out what I was good at and I did it.

And one thing I felt like I really got right, the one thing I was proudest of, was being a father.

So tell me. Answer this for me. How did I – of all people, me?

How did I raise a bully?

Hindsight

I was a bully at his age. I see that now.

I didn't think I was. I thought I was a nice guy. So did my schoolmates. Most of them. And the ones who didn't? The ones who flinched when they saw me coming? They didn't matter. They didn't count.

That's what made it OK. OK to make fun of them. OK to scare them a little. Or maybe even hit them when no one was watching.

Not that I thought of it as hitting. More like rough-housing. A shove in the hallway, a punch on the arm.

All good fun, you know?

Nobody ever told me it was wrong. If anything, they cheered me on. It made me cool. We were the ones that mattered. It helped to have someone who didn't, who always got out of our way.

Someone like my son.

I want to tell him to fight back, to be tough. To deal with it. But I know better. He's not like that. He's never been like that. And I don't want him to be. I love him just like he is. Just like he's been since I first held him in my arms.

So how do I protect him? How do I protect him from people like me?

Guardian

You want to protect your child. You want to put your arms around her and curl your body over her and take any blow the world tries to give her. You want her to wear your love like a cloak, a cloak that will ward off any evil.

But you don't get to be there every minute. You don't get to be on the school bus, you don't get to be in the hallway. You don't get to be out behind the school where the teachers never check.

And when she comes home and you ask if she's alright and she tells you everything's fine, you don't get to peer behind her eyes and see what makes you think it isn't and when she just closes up all the more when you try to coax her out, you don't get to know what is lurking there in her own dark. You don't know what to protect her from.

When she keeps getting sick and not wanting to go to school and looking even sicker when she has to and starts having trouble in class when she was always such a good student and you keep asking if anything's the matter and she starts to avoid you, to spend all her time in her room and there you are, wanting to defend her, wanting to stand up for her, but not knowing what's behind the curtain, what's got her so afraid, until finally, without your ever seeing it, the thing she has to be afraid of, what's most dangerous to her now, is herself, the one being you can never protect her from, and after it's too late, after it's done, all you can think, think over and over again, is, "You failed; you failed to protect your child".

College

Jerome

Guys, you gotta hear this. Last year, there was this freshman on the ground floor. And he kept to himself, just stayed in his room. He'd say hello if you spoke to him, but never quite looked you in the eye, you know?

OK. So one night we got some shrooms. Primo shrooms. And a few of us did them in my room. Then we went downstairs to Schuyler's. He had some vodka, so we drank that and then did more shrooms.

Someone said, "Hey, where's your neighbor?" And Schuyler said, "Where do you think he is? Hibernating. We probably won't see him until next Spring." And we all laughed. But someone else said, "That's rude". And someone else agreed. "Yeah, what's he think we are? Trolls?" And we all began to hunch over and make troll sounds until finally someone said, "Let's scare the bear!" and before we knew it we were all out in the hallway and then we opened this guy's door without even knocking. He was reading and he started to say something but before he could, we all grabbed hold of him and dragged him out in the hallway and started dancing around him chanting, "Let's scare the bear! Let's scare the bear!" And I guess we did. 'Cause all he could do was curl up in a ball, covering his head like he was hoping we wouldn't hurt him.

Which was stupid, right? We weren't going to hurt him. We just wanted to have some fun.

Anyway after a while it got boring, so we left him there and went back to Schuyler's room.

But let me tell you that was funny. We were laughing about it for days.

He left soon after that, at the end of the semester. I wish I could remember the kid's name. What was it again?

Oh yeah. Jerome.

Jerome. Better known as the Bear.

The Rally

Hey, man, Did you hear? There's a rally tonight for Timothy. Over on the Common.

Here's the scoop. Timothy and the other guys in Stone House, they're all really cool. Timothy, he's this super talented musician. And his roommate's a poet. A slam poet. Check him out; he's on line, This one guy, though, Ernie, well, Ernie's the odd man out. Real uptight, stick to the rules, kind of guy. And he wasn't down with some of what was going on. The music late at night. And other stuff.

I mean, they're artists. They party, right?

So he complained, first to them, but of course they blew him off, and then to the Administration. Which is so not cool.

So Timothy decided he needed a nudge. You know, to make him want to change dorms. Nothing bad; it's not like he hurt him or anything. But, say, sometimes Ernie's stuff would disappear. Or one night he got in his bed and someone had taken a dump on the sheets. Funny, huh? Or maybe, late at night, someone would pound on his door and then when he'd get up, they'd be gone.

See what I mean? Jokes, that's all. It's not like anyone got hurt.

Only Ernie, well wouldn't you know it, he went and reported all this, the big damn crybaby, so the school asked around and now they're trying to kick Timothy out.

So all because Ernie's so uncool and on top of which, it was for his own good, he'd really be better off in another dorm, Timothy just thought he'd speed that along, well now they're coming down on Timothy. Which is totally unfair.

So try to make it, OK, to the rally? Because Timothy really needs our support.

Rocket

Oh my God! You're telling me you're a virgin? My own roommate has never had sex? Never? My god, how can you even admit being such a freak?

Seriously, I can't begin to tell you what you're missing. You've never made it with a guy? Wait until I tell Rocket. She'll think it's the funniest thing she's ever heard. Oh come on, I have to tell Rocket; we do everything together. Absolutely everything. She won't believe you've never done it.

'Cause Rocket's experienced. I'm telling you, she's an expert. You wouldn't believe some of the things she's taught me. Do you know, I'd never been on a motorcycle until Rocket took me out? Oh yeah. Just her holding the handlebars and me holding her. And when it broke down? She fixed it. She's good with her hands, let me tell you. She knows all kinds of things. And all kinds of people. But someone our age who's a virgin? Seriously? That's one for the records.

'Cause how can you not want to? Do you know how good a guy can make you feel? I can't begin to tell you what it's like. I wouldn't even know where to start.

What I can tell you, it's embarrassing. It's embarrassing that you, my roommate, haven't done it. That's just not right, Hon'. You've got to get with the program. You've got to be like everyone else. 'Cause otherwise people are going to start looking at you funny, and then that's going to rub off on me. And people will start talking about you; about you and me. And me and Rocket. And I really don't want that.

I don't want people talking about me and Rocket just because you're such a freak.

You Can Tell

She must be a lesbian. That's why she's so weird. Even her hair. It never looks quite right. Oh sure it's girly enough, but that doesn't mean anything. They don't all have short hair, you know. And don't be fooled. When she says how she wishes she was pretty so she could meet a guy, that's just something they say. So people won't know. You can't go by that.

All you have to do is look at her. She's not, you know, like the rest of us. Not playing to the same beat. Not hip to the program. Oh she's friendly enough. It's not like she badmouths people or anything.

Which I hate. I hate when people talk about other people behind their back.

She's just, I don't know, out of synch.

Like how she laughs. Have you ever heard her laugh? Always too quick. And tense. Tight. Not like a laugh at all. More like she's scared.

Scared of what, for Pete's sake? Us?

That laugh really works my nerves.

Not that I hang out with her much. No one does. Not even her roommate. She pretty much steers clear of her. Most people do. Not in a mean way. Don't get me wrong. This isn't high school, for Gods-sakes. It's not like we're some kind of clique. It's just, what can I say, she's strange.

That's why I think she must be, you know, that way. Or maybe she isn't. Anyway that's not what matters. Not to me. All that matters, OK, is that she's weird.

Clothes

Where'd you get that shirt? From a cut-out bin? And those jeans? "Cavin Kein"? Seriously?

C'mon. You're smart, right? You must be, with all those scholarships. So you see it, right? You've gotta see that other people don't dress like that.

And please, spare me your usual line about, "I don't have the money." You worry way too much about money, Man. Why don"t you just ask your parents for a credit card? That's what I did. How do you think I got to Cabo?

Ask them. What? Are you afraid you'll embarrass them? Put them on the spot? C'mon. It's not like they're paying for your education, right? You're on a full scholarship, for Pete's sake. Just tell them how it is: that there's more to college than getting good grades. You want to fit in; you want to dress the part.

'Cause, right now, you look like one of those kids my church used to send to summer camp. They'd pass around a picture and say, "Help this poor kid get out of the projects. If only for the summer."

Seriously man, that's what you look like, man. Exactly like one of those kids.

You don't want people thinking you're a charity case, do you? So get some new clothes already. Just do it. Stop worrying so much about money.

Take it from me, Man. Money is no big deal.

Sisters

Whap!

We took their pants down. Whap!

No cute little shorts or designer jeans. Whap! That's for when you're a sister. Whap! When you're in. Whap! Whap! Whap! When you're one of us.

After the initiation.

Becka, she's the pretty one. Whap! I wanted her. Whap! She's the one who cared the least if she got in. Why should she? She'd be popular anyway. Whap! It's only because her mother was in, and her older sister. Whap! That's why she went along. That's why she let us do this. "C'mon,", I said – Whap! - "It's just a spanking, you big baby!" 'Cause she wanted to cry, I could see that, each time the paddle landed. Whap! Whap! Whap! She wanted to let it out. But she didn't, not even when the welts came up; not even when there was blood. Whap! Whap! "So, you want to be a sister?" Whap! "You think you're good enough?" Whap! "You want to be one of us!" Whap!

There was blood on the paddle now. I know I should have stopped, but I was waiting for her to ask. Whap! I was waiting for her to beg! Whap! I wanted her to know she wasn't better. Whap! To never forget that I was in charge, that no matter how many guys looked at her – Whap! – I'd always be the one, the one she let do this to her.

But she didn't cry out and she didn't give in; she didn't tell me that I was better than her. Instead... she fainted. Just straight up fainted, slumping against the wall. Even then I kept hitting her, watching the blood spread, until finally one of the others stopped me, and said we'd better get out of there.

But I don't know why everyone's so angry. It's not like she won't recover. And anyway, she asked for it, didn't she? That's what she agreed to; that's what she signed on for, when she said she wanted to be a sister.

Thinking

Did his parents come pick up his stuff? I thought of being there. To apologize. But they don't want to see me. I know they don't.

Can you blame them?

Look, I want you to know, it was never about how he was. That didn't matter to me. I liked the guy. I liked him fine. Sure, I knew he'd be embarrassed, once the video hit the Net. But that was it, you know? Embarrassed.

I never would have guessed. I never would have thought he'd take it so hard.

My parents heard it on the news. Before I could call them. They were so proud when I got in here. They didn't mind having to scrape up the tuition. Even though it's hard for them. Really hard.

My dad was so quiet. He just said, "So, where do you go from here?" Letting me know. Letting me know I'm on my own now.

There'll probably be a lawsuit, huh? Not right away. After the funeral. After they've had some time.

So I'll have to think about that. When it happens. For now I have to figure out where to transfer. If any school will take me.

It's so much to think about.

If only I'd thought as hard before. Before I played that stupid joke.

The Adult World

Troll

I'm just a screen name to you. One more person posting on-line. You don't know what I look like, you don't know who I am.

You just know I'm mean. I don't know you either, I've never even met you, but I know just enough about you to get under your skin. To make you afraid to speak out. Why bother? You know I'll jump on you. You know I'll call you an idiot, or catch you in an error, or twist what you say just enough that you sound like the mean one, you sound like you're trying to start something. It doesn't matter that you didn't exactly say that; you know no one will go back and check. And so you try to defend yourself, and then I tell you to stop getting upset, and that gets to you some more, really, really gets to you, that and how mean I sound, just out-of-the-blue, no explanation, just because, mean, and maybe that's what's most upsetting, that there's no reason behind it, that you can't understand how much hostility can fit into so few words, and why, and that's so hard to take, isn't it, how crazy it is, how irrational and the next thing you know you're coming back at me, back at me hard, and you don't even know what you're typing, and all the people reading you, all the people who started out on your side, they start to get embarrassed for you, they start to think you're going too far, because you've lost it now, haven't you, you've lost it completely.

And me?

Me, I've won.

The Hard Knock of Opportunity

Didn't I trust you? Didn't I give you a chance? I could have managed those programmers myself; you know I could. You think I got to be the boss by accident? But I gave you an opportunity. That's what you have to understand. I gave you a chance to show what you can do.

Which, it turns out, isn't much. Wouldn't you agree? Am I wrong?

If I'm wrong, just tell me. Go ahead and tell me.

And don't go telling me it's because I was always stepping in. I had to get involved, didn't I? Because you just weren't cutting it. But it's still your responsibility.

Don't go trying to shift this mess.

What am I supposed to tell the client? Don't you think he's going to blame me? Of course he will. Only, don't kid yourself. He knows I put you in charge; he knows I try to give my people a chance. Because that's what a good manager does. And I'm a good manager.

You'd agree with that, right? You wouldn't say any different, would you?

The client knows that, for sure. He knows I'm trying to help you. To make you better.

So yeah, it's my tail on the line, but don't kid yourself. He knows why we're behind schedule; he knows who to blame. So if he tells me to cut you loose, well, I'm sorry. There's only so much I can do. But the fact is, we're in it. In it deep. And whose fault do you think that is?

I'll tell you one thing: it's not mine.

With My Little Ax

Don't get me wrong, Jack. I like Stu. Everybody likes Stu. Whenever the guys in the group go out, he's the first one they ask. Like it wouldn't be the same without him. The clients like him too. He's really popular.

And sure, he's good at what he does. As far as it goes. But here's the thing: how far does it? Can he ever be more than a worker bee? And what about it? What about his being so nice?

If you make him project manager, he's going to have to make some tough choices. Things that won't be popular. You think he's got that in him? Especially with him being friends with everyone in the group?

I just don't see any vision there, any larger view. Sure, he does the job. He's completely into the job. That's part of the problem. He's not looking ahead. He's not working the angles. He just takes things as they come.

I don't know. That's not how I'd do it. You've got to be political. You've got to lay some groundwork. That's just reality.

Now I realize this might mean losing him. He might not take it well. And that's a shame. Because like I said, he does what he does well. As far as it goes.

It's just, promoting him? Moving him to the next level? That would be a big mistake.

But don't get me wrong. I like the guy. I really, really like the guy.

The Lizard Queen

Twenty-five? Come on. Add a decade to that and you might be close.

Let me tell you, Elly hates her. Just between you and me, Elly had her hopes regarding Conrad. That's a laugh, huh? I like Elly, but let's face it, even if she lost a few pounds, Conrad would be way out of her league. The important thing is, Elly's got the Web skills. Oh, I've may have a PhD, but that stuff's way beyond me. Damian and I, we're the wordsmiths; the "content providers", I believe is the term of art. And there's others. Trust me. Lots of people have it out for this chick.

But Elly especially. Right from the start, she just loved the idea. Went right to work on our subject's picture, adding scales up and down her neck and a reptile tongue flicking out of her mouth.

Oh yeah, because what we're calling the Web page is: "The Lizard Queen". Catchy, huh? Not that the... uh... girl is exactly svelte – you know Conrad went for that chest, it sure wasn't her brains – but somehow "Lizard Queen" suits her. 'Cause she creeps us all out. For Gods-sake, she's almost as old as Damian, yet here she is acting all girly and jejune.

It just makes my skin crawl. So, yeah, "Lizard Queen" it is.

It's taken us some time because, hey, we're grown-ups, right? We have jobs, responsibilities. So this has been like a side project. A labor of hate, you might say. Damian got some ideas from his students. (You know how mean teens can be, right? Trust me, you did not want to be me in high school.) So I took some of those and whipped up some of my own. I did my thesis on satire, you know. So I learned from the masters: Jonathan Swift, Mark Twain.

I'm telling you, this stuff is top shelf.

So now, between the picture and a few well-chosen words, oh yeah, and some stuff we dug up about her from around the Web (it's amazing what's out there if you look), we're ready to unleash our reptile on the world.

Here, let me show you the page. Man, I'm telling you: I wish I could see her face the first time she sees this page.

The Second Lesson

We put you on the spot, didn't we? About who gets the office. I know I thought I was just making my case, laying out the facts, straight and plain. But you could tell, couldn't you? You could tell there was more to it for me.

Here's the thing. I told you once how I hated high school, how I was one of the kids people picked on. What I never told you was why it all stopped. All at once.

One day this kid, one of the nastier ones, started in on me. Exactly like he had a bunch of times before. Only this time, it was like a switch flipped inside me. I decided I wasn't going to take it. Just like that. So instead of covering my head like he expected, or trying to get away, I hit him back. And he couldn't believe it. Oh, he knocked me around a bit. But that didn't stop me. Because I'd made up my mind. And he could see that. He could see that, this time, I was going to stand my ground.

And that was that. He turned and walked away.

That was an amazing day for me. Amazing. I learned you could win just by standing your ground. By showing you weren't about to walk away. And don't think I used that just in high school.

There are bullies everywhere. Even here, here in the business world.

So I'm glad I learned that lesson and I'm glad I learned it young. But it's taken me too long to learn another one. The truth is, I don't care about that office. I just resented having to give way, to let someone else get over me. And like I said, I learned a long time ago not to do that.

What I'm saying is, give Cal the office. Because if there's one thing I should have learned by now, the second lesson I needed to take to heart, it's when not to let your past be your present. When it's time to walk away from a fight.

Car

It was just like a real car. At least to a six-year-old. Low to the ground and made of blue metal and when I sat down in it and pedaled, I felt as grown-up as could be, tooling around the sidewalk.

So you can imagine how proud I felt when two older kids came up and checked it out. "That's some wheels you got there, buddy." I didn't know these kids; they weren't from the neighborhood. They looked pretty tough. But then so did a lot of our neighbors.

I got out so one of them could take a look at it. Meanwhile, the other kid was super friendly. He started talking to me about his dad's red sports car. "It's right down the block," he said and pointed behind me. I turned around, but I couldn't see it. I felt stupid because he kept pointing and saying it was right there, I just had to look harder.

Then I remembered my car.

I turned around and it was gone. The kid next to me punched me on the arm with this ugly grin, then took off running.

I started crying and running after him. But of course I was too little. And the other kids, the kids from the neighborhood? They just laughed.

The more I cried, the more they laughed.

I've dealt with a lot of crap over the years and more often than not I've come out on top. So maybe I should be grateful to those kids, grateful for showing me early how mean the world can be. But if anything, the older I get, the angrier I get when I think about it.

I mean, I was six. What kind of person steals from a six-year-old? And what kind of person laughs at him? Laughs while he's crying his heart out.

The thing is, you may learn from it, you may get past it, but you don't forget it.

You don't ever forget it.

Made in the USA
Charleston, SC
24 April 2015